DEER

NORTH AMERICAN ANIMAL DISCOVERY LIBRARY

Lynn M. Stone

Rourke Corporation, Inc.
Vero Beach, Florida 32964

PHOTO CREDITS

All photos by author

LIBRARY OF CONGRESS
Library of Congress Cataloging-in-Publication Data
Stone, Lynn M., 1942-
  Deer / by Lynn M. Stone.

    p. cm. — (North American animal discovery library)
    Summary: An introduction to the physical characteristics,
habits, and natural environment, and future prospects of the
two species of North American deer.
    ISBN 0-86593-043-0
    1. Deer—Juvenile literature. [1. Deer.] I. Title.
II. Series: Stone, Lynn M., 1942- North American animal
discovery library.
QL737.U55S76   1990
599.73'57—dc20   89-70172
                          CIP
Printed in the USA   AC

Deer

TABLE OF CONTENTS

THE DEER

How would it feel to carry a coat rack on your head? If you were a male deer, you would know.

Deer are the best known of North America's large, hooved, wild animals. Male deer don't really wear coat racks, but they do have **antlers.**

Antlers are something like a coat rack because they stick out and they are rock hard.

Two kinds, or **species,** of deer live in North America. They are the white-tailed deer *(Odocoileus virginianus)* and the mule deer *(Odocoileus hemionus).*

Mule Deer in "Velvet"

THE DEER'S COUSINS

White-tailed and mule deer are closely related to other members of the deer family. All male members of the deer family carry antlers.

The moose is the largest member of the deer family in the world. A male, or bull, moose may weigh 1,400 pounds.

Moose have broad, flattened antlers.

The elk is also much larger than the deer. Bull elks have thick necks and huge, spreading antlers.

Caribou are deer that live mostly in Alaska and northern Canada. This deer is closely related to the reindeer of northern Europe.

Bull elk

HOW THEY LOOK

Deer are brown or gray with black-and-white trim. Deer have long legs and big, dark eyes.

Antlers grow early in summer. They are at first covered by tiny hairs which form a velvet blanket.

Mule deer bucks average about 250 pounds. Females, called **does,** are smaller. White-tailed deer are generally smaller than mule deer.

Mule deer have black tails. They also have wider antlers and longer ears than whitetails.

Whitetail doe

WHERE THEY LIVE

Each species of animal lives in an area called its **range.** The mule deer's range covers western Canada south through the western United States and east to Minnesota and western Texas.

The whitetail's range includes southern Canada and most of the United States. The whitetail's range continues south into South America.

Within a range, deer live on certain types of land. These places are their **habitat.** Mule deer like the edges of forest and brush in mountains and hills. Whitetails like forest edges, farmland, and open woodland.

Mule Deer, Washington State

Mule Deer fawn

Whitetailed Deer

HOW THEY LIVE

Bucks and does spend most of the year apart. However, during the autumn mating season they are together. Deer also band together in winter.

Bucks often fight with each other in the fall. A buck may chase another male away from does, or the two may duel with their antlers.

Deer are most active in the early morning and in the evening. During the day, hidden in a shady spot, they rest.

Deer are good swimmers and fast, graceful runners.

Shed antler

THE DEER'S FAWNS

Mother deer have one or two babies, called **fawns.**

Fawns weigh from four and one-half to seven pounds at birth.

Fawns are spotted. The spots help them hide in the leaves and twigs of the forest floor. A fawn can stand 10 minutes after birth, but it is safer for the fawn not to move about.

Deer that survive hunters, disease, and being struck by cars can live several years. Deer in captivity have lived to age 20.

*Whitetailed fawn
and doe*

PREDATOR AND PREY

Deer are called **herbivores,** because they eat plants. Deer eat soft, green plants and berries, leaves, twigs, and acorns.

Deer are **prey,** or food, for the large, meat-eating animals known as **predators.** These meat eaters usually eat sick, injured, young, or very old deer. Cougars (mountain lions), bears, wolves, and coyotes all kill deer now and then.

Deer have good eyes and ears to warn them of danger. They also have sharp hooves and antlers with which to defend themselves.

Wolf and deer

DEER AND PEOPLE

Many wild animals have disappeared during this century. The growth of cities and farms had destroyed their habitats.

Deer, however, have not suffered. Mule deer are common in the West. White-tailed deer are common in the East.

Now there are more white-tailed deer than before.

White-tailed deer love farm crops, and they can live in forest or brush close to cities.

Deer are **game** animals. They are hunted with gun or bow and arrow during certain times each year.

Key Deer, Florida

THE DEER'S FUTURE

Hunting laws and the loss of predators that eat deer have helped deer.

Key deer are a type of white-tailed deer. They are about the size of a large dog. Key deer live only on a few of the islands, or keys, off the southern tip of Florida. Key deer have lost much of their habitat, and they are becoming scarce.

Most deer herds, though, have a bright future. Deer live in places today where they were never seen before.

Glossary

antlers (ANT lers)—the sharp, bony growths on the heads of male deer

doe (DOE)—a female deer

fawn (FAWN)—a baby deer

game (GAME)—animals that are hunted for sport

habitat (HAB a tat)—the kind of place in which an animal lives, such as a woodland

herbivore (ERB a vore)—an animal that eats plants

predator (PRED a tor)—an animal that kills other animals for food

prey (PRAY)—an animal that is hunted by another for food

range (RAYNJ)—the entire area in which a certain type of animal lives

species (SPEE sheez)—within a group of closely related animals, one certain kind

INDEX